BEYOND HAIKU

WOMEN PILOTS WRITE POETRY

**FIG
FACTOR
MEDIA**

ISBN: 978-1-952779-03-9
Library of Congress Control Number: 2021917090

BEYOND HAIKU

WOMEN PILOTS WRITE POETRY

CAPTAIN LINDA PAUWELS

III

DEDICATION

To the princesses of long ago, who sported wings hidden under gentian gowns.[1]

---

[1][See poem "Moyen Age," p. 23-Ed.]

Carpent tua poma nepotes.[2]

–Virgil

---

[2][Translation: Your descendants shall gather your fruits-Ed.]

TABLE OF CONTENTS

FOREWORD

By Christine Negroni

At least once a day, and usually more often, I whip out my cell phone and take a picture. I bet you do, too. In 2020, nearly one and a half trillion photos were taken and not with conventional cameras either—the vast majority were recorded on the billions of cell phones that are never far from reach.

Taking a photo is my attempt to turn the fleeting into something permanent. This is why I was quite unsettled one night when I was out in Cadaqués, Spain, without my cell phone. I was on the Costa Brava to write a story about the places that inspired great works of art. Cadaqués, the home of Salvador Dali, was frequently featured in Dali's paintings and sculptures.

As I walked home from dinner in the city center, I passed by a quiet harbor with an enormous silver globe of a moon bouncing its reflection off the lightly ruffled surface of the Mediterranean.

Scenes like this inspired Dali's art. But I am not an artist.

"To own this scene," I thought to myself, "I'm going to have to capture it in words." Balancing between wild appreciation of the view and mad frustration with my inability to contain it in pixels, I pulled out my notebook and began to write.

To my surprise, when I returned to the United States and read what I wrote that night, I had a startlingly clear memory of what I saw and more. I could hear again the clanking of metal grommets on the masts of the sailboats, and I could feel the temperature of the breeze on my face.

The writer/philosopher Alain de Botton once told me that when we try to recreate what we see, we go from observing things in a loose way to a deeper and more nuanced view of the component parts. Whether it is drawing or writing doesn't matter; the act of observation, concentration and duplication enriches the memories as we are making them so they are more potent on recall.

The ubiquity of cell phone cameras puts us in a conundrum tempting us to snap away while interfering with the process of really seeing.

For pilots—as well as midwives, astronomers, marine biologists, and others whose professional lives allow them to see exceptional things—the desire to capture their experiences must seem overwhelming. For those whose work appears in these pages, poetry is the solution.

In *Beyond Haiku: Women Pilots Write Poetry*, the poets have preserved what they see, hear, smell and feel in words that are richer than any image. Because while a photo captures a moment, a poem captures emotions.

A poem by Kathy Shelton revolves around an ordinary scene, a pilot preparing for flight glancing at her iPad—and what she sees will touch your heart. In her little-known poem, "From an Airplane," Amelia Earhart recounts in a single sunset the allure of flight.

So set down your cellphone and turn the page; a mosaic of multi-sensory word images awaits.

Christine Negroni is an aviation and travel writer and the author of two books on aviation safety. Her most recent book, The Crash Detectives: Investigating the World's Most Mysterious Air Disasters, *is a* New York Times *Bestseller. Find her at www.christinenegroni.com.*

ACKNOWLEDGEMENTS

This book would not exist but for a seed planted by retired American Airlines Captain Stephen Walton. After *Beyond Haiku: Pilots Write Poetry* was published last year, I promised myself I'd be done with writing. Stephen, your comment of "Linda, you have at least two more books in you" lit the match. I'm not certain I should be thanking you yet. *Odi et amo.*

As with any seed, creativity needs fertile soil to germinate. Thank you, Elizabeth Booker of Aviatrix Book Review, for tilling the field during your author interview. Answering your questions allowed me to fully articulate my vision for this book and the Beyond Haiku series. Your continued support means a lot to me.

Once planted, this little seed was cared for by publisher Jacqueline Ruiz and her team at Fig Factor Media. Project manager Gabriela Hernández Franch worked closely with me from day one to ensure a beautiful book would ultimately blossom. Editor Michele Kelly provided guidance and commentary, so I could continue to refine the craft of writing. Christine Borges proofread the manuscript and took time on a Saturday morning to jointly review the numerous footnotes and bibliography for correctness. Designer Manuel Serna used his artistic eye to place the images and illustrations onto these pages for your enjoyment. To the entire team: please accept my sincerest appreciation.

Early on, artist Priscilla Patterson of the American Society of Aviation Artists misted this sproutling with life-giving water. Thank you, Priscilla, for mentoring young artists and for your pencil portraits of Bohn, Earhart, Ramsey, and Thaden. Your collaboration has elevated this project. It would not be the same without you.

Thank you to artists Lynsey Steinberg, for designing and gifting us an amazing book cover, and Callista Chabot, for perfectly imbuing our cover illustration with an *aha* moment!

Thank you, artists Sloan Alley, Rebecca Peitz, and Skye Stauffer, of the "Secret Poet Society," for understanding that loose lips sink ships and for keeping our secret tight. Thank you, Sophia Downard, for the soft touch and care you used to illustrate a haiku arising from tragic circumstances.

To archivists Kate Igoe of the Smithsonian, Sammie Morris of Purdue, and Patrizia Nava of UT Dallas, thank you for being the keepers of our aviation history and for helping me bring words from our celebrated past back into the sunlight.

As we prepared this budding bloom for market, I relied on the kindness of communications professional and student pilot Anthony Flynn and author and retired pilot Byron Edgington, who took the time to beta read the manuscript and provided suggestions and opinions. Thank you, Anthony and Byron. Two of my pilot colleagues, American Airlines Captain Terri McCallister and First Officer Sheryl Rogers, came in as reinforcements, along with Argentine professor and translator Erika Zausi, to assist with collecting bios and photos of contributing authors and artists for the book's website. Thank you, Terri, Sheryl, and Erika.

The seed as a metaphor has been used since antiquity. It exemplifies the power of potential, its individual components remaining distinct even as they unify and then merge to create a whole. To the fifty-eight contributing authors and thirty-one artists, each and every word and illustration in this book retains a unique part of who you are. Thank you for sharing of yourselves for the benefit of the whole.

I close with love and gratitude to my husband Frederick, a man of action who gave me wide space to write, knowing how thorny things can get in the land of words.

Linda Pauwels

INTRODUCTION

When it comes to flying, there is a process for everything. It starts with the preflight. The pilot assesses her own fitness to fly; evaluates the conditions for departure, arrival, and route of flight; physically inspects the aircraft and equipment; and briefs the passengers and crew. Then, the before—start checklist is accomplished. With a big breath in,[3] the engine comes to life—and the journey begins. *Beyond Haiku: Women Pilots Write Poetry*, the second book in the *Beyond Haiku* series, is a shared creative expression of life on this journey. It continues the concept mapped out in the first book, *Pilots Write Poetry*, in which pilot-composed haiku gave readers a unique glimpse into the flying life.

Within these pages, you will find original works composed by fifty-eight women aviators of diverse flying backgrounds and ages, from a high school student to octogenarians, from ten different countries. Three happen to be women pilots from an earlier time: Amelia Earhart, Louise Thaden, and Delphine Bohn. Most of the poems were received following a request for submissions issued in December 2020 and disseminated through major women pilot organizations.

Although the poetry submission request specified a maximum of three original haiku or short poems, some longer poems were received. In order to maintain harmony with the principle "all are welcome here,"[4] I incorporated work by every contributor, even using excerpts of the longer poems, and curated these elements into a cohesive whole. A list of contributing authors is located on page 110. Additional information about the authors may be found on the book's website, www.beyondhaiku.com.

One by one, as the poems arrived, a remarkable commonality of feelings about flying emerged. Trained in journalism, I sensed a larger story, and thus began digging. Historical research validated my intuition. It led to the discovery that Amelia Earhart "secretly dreamed of becoming an accomplished creative writer... she wrote numerous poems and drafts of short stories; the majority

---

[3] Linda Pauwels, "Jet's Thrust Starts with a Big Breath In," in *The Orange County Register*, May 30, 2004.
[4] Kosaka, Kitaro, director. 2018. *Okko's Inn*. Dream Link Entertainment (DLE).

of these efforts were written before she became a famous aviator."[5] Many of her writings have not seen the light of day.

Notably, eight of Earhart's poems dating from the early 1920s are contained in this book, published with permission of the Purdue Research Foundation. Also, aviation pioneer Louise Thaden's poem, composed after her first solo flight in 1927, is printed here with the permission of the Smithsonian National Air and Space Museum. Excerpts of WWII poems clipped by WASF Delphine Bohn, from one of her scrapbooks located at the University of Texas at Dallas archives, are featured as well.

These voices from aviation's storied past join those of us flying today to create a collective meditation[6] on themes important to women pilots: strength and endurance, radiance and beauty, love of flying, and finding balance. Mindful of the importance of paying homage to the genre, each chapter begins with a haiku from a poet traditionally recognized as a master of haiku.

Alongside the shared poetic effort, and of equal creative weight, is the artwork adorning the pages of *Women Pilots Write Poetry*. Illustrations are by six adult artists and twenty-six young artists ages seven to seventeen who are children of pilots, or of those who provide close support to pilots. More information about these artists and the beautiful artwork in this book, including the cover and four cameo portraits, is found in the Illustration Credits section on page 115.

All proceeds from *Women Pilots Write Poetry* will directly fund aviation scholarships.[7] May those young women, who as little girls saw contrails like the ribbons in their hair fluttering down, learn to fly and come to love the sky.[8]

[5]Sammie L. Morris, "What Archives Reveal: The Hidden Poems of Amelia Earhart," in *Libraries Research Publications*, Paper 28, 2006.
[6]Samantha David, personal email to the author, February 12, 2021.
[7][Proceeds will be donated to ISA+21, The Ninety-Nines, Women in Aviation International, Miami-Dade College Eig-Watson School of Aviation, and The American Society of Aviation Artists-Ed.]]
[8]Mary Jo Zignego, message to the author, posted on 'The Line' pilot forum, June 11, 2021.

Explanatory Note on Amelia Earhart's Poems

As a young woman growing up in the 1970s and 1980s, I looked for female role models in my history books. I recall there were very few, but there was one bright and shining exception, a woman whose courage and adventurous spirit continues to captivate children of all ages: Amelia Earhart.

In 2003, I accepted my dream job of working with Earhart's archival papers and memorabilia housed at Purdue University. One of my primary goals, in addition to organizing and preserving these important papers, was to get to know Earhart more fully by studying her writings. To my surprise, I found that there was a small collection of poems mixed in with her papers, most of which had never been published.

Many people are unaware that Amelia Earhart wrote poetry. She had one poem, "Courage," published in her lifetime without her consent. Unfortunately, many of her writings have been lost to time, and the small set of poems in her papers at Purdue are the only known poems of hers that exist. These poems help us understand Earhart and reveal an intimate glimpse into her private thoughts.

She wrote about love, sorrow, and flight. She was particularly inspired by the beauty of clouds, and the quiet serenity she found flying high above the earth. As I read through the poems Linda Pauwels has curated for this book, I couldn't help noticing that Earhart and Pauwels share common goals: to inspire and empower young people—particularly young women—to pursue their dreams. Women's rights have expanded since Earhart's time, but there are still barriers for women in many male-dominated fields.

When I imagine readers picking up this book, I picture the smiles and excitement on their faces. There is just something poetic about flight that cannot be denied. It inspires big dreams, romantic yearnings, creativity, and a desire to make one's mark on the world. By focusing this volume on women pilots, Pauwels has ensured that the perspectives of women pilots are part of our understanding of what it means to be a pilot and a poet. I believe Amelia Earhart and her contemporaries would be proud of this beautiful, inspirational book. Happy reading!

Sammie L. Morris
Professor and Director of the Virginia Kelly Karnes Research Center
Purdue University Libraries

1) STRENGTH AND ENDURANCE

Little snail
Inch by inch, climb
Mount Fuji!

–Kobayashi Issa (1763-1828)[9]

---

[9]David G. Lanoue, "Haiku of Kobayashi Issa," http://haikuguy.com/issa.

Carol Scherer was twelve years old when, as a member of the Eugene Obsidians Club, she climbed her first mountain, the 10,358-foot South Sister in Oregon. Over the next five summers, mentored in climbing skills and disciplines by expert mountaineer Norman Wallace Benton, she would summit most of the peaks in the Northwest.

"From those climbs," Scherer noted, "I learned that you can do more than you think you can. You can't give up, teamwork is essential, and even the strongest knees shake on a steep slope with avalanches. You have to stay calm and focused and keep moving."

These lessons from her teens helped Carol feel comfortable in aviation too. Her childhood dream of becoming a pilot, "not a woman pilot, or a female pilot," took flight on wings of readiness and determination. And as it came to pass, Carol had the historical distinction of being part of UPT 77-08, the first class of ten women officers to graduate from the U.S. Air Force Undergraduate Pilot Training Program. Then, after serving twelve years in the Air Force, Scherer flew for thirty years as a pilot for American Airlines.

A pilot's climb to the summit can be long and hard. Looking back with the perspective of a professional aviator, she stated: "It's a lifestyle that is demanding and often physical. Being up all night and still attentive. Making decisions in stressful situations and following through with your plans. Year after year. For decades."[10]

Captain Pauwels wrote the above introduction based on a personal interview with Carol Scherer.

---

[10]Carol Scherer, emails to the author, May 21-23, 2021.

To snatch molten moments from
The fire of life
Holding them until the brief
Glow fades, and they are hardened
To their everlasting shape

–Amelia Earhart[11]

[11] Notes for an untitled poem, b6f100i1, George Palmer Putnam collection of Amelia Earhart papers, MSP 9, Purdue University Archives and Special Collections, Purdue University Libraries.

You too can fly a plane
Unless you're timid, doubtful
And unambitious

-Leslie Nixon

When first learning to fly
It quite boggles the mind
So, students make sure
Your instructor is kind

-Suzanne Ramsey, from "On Obtaining a Pilot License"

"You're too small to fly"
"I don't have to lift the plane"
Aerodynamics

-Donna Miller

Fly the plane like life
Dark skies or fair skies ahead
Pilot's vigilance

-Elizabeth Hawley

So many hues of blue, I can't begin to Name
all the colors
And then, there's the world below...
It's never looked so clear
The sky is my home
Every price I paid to get here
Was worth it

-Syd Blue, from "Why Fly?"

The sun shines so high
My dreams are persistent as lotus seeds
Strengthening me to shine higher

-Maciel Mejía

Solo flight
Today is the day
Aligned with runway three five
Eager and alone

-Shakar Soltani

Full power, lift off
Circuit height, lone
Land, taxi stop.
Legs shake
First solo

–Delia Jones

Have you ever been hung by your feet from a rope?
Then twirled all about with your heart in your throat?
The ground's coming up, it's spinning all 'round
Not quite! It's the opposite… it's you going down!

–Suzanne Ramsey, from "On Obtaining a Pilot License"

What lies ahead then?
Students racing through ratings
Will time heal these wounds?

–Nathalie Pauwels

Mr. Check Airman
Please do not test me anymore
My brain hurts too much

-Terri McCallister

The examiner's nickname was "Big Bad Chase"
After passing my challenging check ride
I had an enormous smile on my face

-Kathy Shelton, from "Eighteen"

When we fail, people try to crush our dreams
But once we start to fly,
The skies forget our every failure
And remember how we try

-Madeline Ungurain, from "Soar"

Shall I stay grounded
Or make my return skyward?
Time to vector on

-Raquel Oliva

My flying days are over
My helmet's laid away
My wings are clipped close to my sides
My dreams have gone astray
No longer can I... like the gull
Soar, dive and fly
No longer can I chase the clouds
Chained to earth... am I

–Delphine Bohn[12] papers, from "Wash Out" poem by Pvt. A.R. Petrucci

---

[12]Delphine Bohn Papers, Scrapbook, Box 2, Folder 4, H069-82, History of Aviation Collection, Special Collections Department, Eugene McDermott Library, The University of Texas at Dallas.

Then you got nasty:
"You'll crash and you'll die
You don't understand
You're flying like pastry
You're stubborn and deaf
You'll never succeed
License what license
That's not what you need"

You never let up
You wasted your time
You spoke to thin air
Cos I have my license
I'm where I belong
I am a pilot
And you
You were wrong

-Samantha David, "My First Flying Instructor"

The instructor threw up his hands
He said you have control
I grabbed the cyclic and collective
And tried hard not to roll

But this was work, a tug, a jerk
A full-on helmet fire
Could I succeed at this great deed?
To hover this big gyre?

Many years and hundreds of hours
Have passed since I first tried
But now with skill and precision
A helo I do fly

-Elizabeth Booker, from "Learning to Hover"

Loud engines rumble
Speed increasing rapidly
Rotate and liftoff

-Erica Schletz

Bumping along
No smooth rides anywhere
Night flight to Dallas

-Holly Beckwith

I hear her announce
This is your Captain speaking
Trailblazing the way

—Shakar Soltani

He has a new boat
And a house on the coast
I have one too
But his cost the most

His children are perfect
And so is his wife
His dog is expensive
What a charmed life

He's talked for hours
All about him, you see
And all through the flight
Not a question about me

—Terri McCallister, from "Captain Me"

Nor'easter rages
Churning belly of monster
Escape, safe landing

-Megan Farley

The safety line,
Drawn in the sand
Blows with the wind
At management's hand

-Karlene Petitt, from "Safety Culture"

The mistakes you make at this late date
They land you in a kind of jail
From which there is no escape, no road
No one has left you a trail

-Terri McCallister, from "On the Lips of Angels"

Wright Flyer at Kill Devil
Perseverance at Jezero Crater
Many sorties in between

-Susan McDonald

We're leaving Khartoum by the light of the moon
We're flying by night and by day
We're out in the heat and we've nothing to eat
Cos we've thrown all our rations away

–Delphine Bohn[13] *papers, from untitled WWII poem*[14]

[13]Delphine Bohn papers.
[14]Gavin Lyall, *Freedom's Battle Volume II: The War in the Air 1939-1945* (London: Hutchinson Random House, 2007), 70.

And when in adverse weather
The winds are all to hell
The navigator's balled-up
The wireless balled as well
We think of all the popsies
We've known in days gone by
And cursed the silly effers
Who taught us how to fly

–Delphine Bohn[15] papers, from untitled WWII poem[16]

[15]Delphine Bohn papers.
[16]Gavin Lyall, 185.

2) Radiance and Beauty

I am nobody
A red sinking autumn sun
Took my name away

–Richard Wright (1908-1960)[17]

[17]Richard Wright, *Haiku: This Other World* (New York: Arcade Publishing, 1998), 1.

The pilot identity is strong. It can often take center stage, especially if one flies for a living. Fortunately, every pilot has at one time or another lost themselves in the vastness of the firmament, feeling so very small in the grand scheme of things.

For a short while, this realization helps keep us in check. Sometimes, it even serves to lift the veil, uncovering our innate capacity to see beauty everywhere.

The selections in this chapter are reflections on inner and outer beauty: of the self, nature, and that which is man-made.

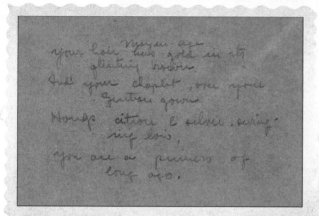

Your hair has gold in its
Glinting brown
And your chaplet, over your gentian gown
Hangs citron & silver,
Swinging low
You are a princess of
Long ago

–Amelia Earhart, "Moyen Age"[18]

---

[18]Amelia Earhart papers, image number b6f104i6.

My warrior princess
Born in spring
Skin peaches and cream

-Linda Pauwels

I'm quite average but
I'm prettier when I fly
It's a special smile

-Donna Miller

I know I look plain
But I am queen of the sky
My duty, to fly

-Jessica Toddun

On a wing to my King
Love to sing and soar
That's what I was put on earth for

-Beth Fielder

Scrambled egg hat
Covers my gray
Four stripes

-Linda Pauwels

I glanced at my iPad
To retrieve information on my arrival airport
I knew the landing would not take long
The runway was quite short
That's when I caught a glimpse of my reflection…
Four stripes and all
Even though I'm of average height
I felt extremely tall

-Kathy Shelton, from "Reflections"

Time, joy, and tears
Intertwined—
Looking glass

–Linda Pauwels

26

There is something irresistible
To me
About that ball of fluff
Those mini parachutes of down
Just waiting for a ride
The wind can take them
Anywhere

–Laureen Miklos, from "Dandelion"

Que tus orquídeas florezcan todas juntas
Por primera vez en la vida
Un amanecer sostenido visto desde la cabina
Un río corriendo frío, entre tus pies desnudos
En primavera
La poesía
Siempre nos salva la poesía

–Lucía Aránega Abellán

Stunning, beautiful, graceful
Wings flexing on every takeoff
She is direct and particular
Procedures done her way
Ensuring a start of a very good day
You must do as she wishes
In the right sequence
Set all of her switches
A highly intelligent, flying computer
When ailing, she'll tell the mechanic why
Eager she is, to get back to the sky
She is sleek, powerful, and fuel-efficient
Compared to her competition
Who could be deemed highly inefficient
The 787
The princess of the sky
If you don't believe it
Just watch her fly!

–Karlene Petitt

On silver wings
Dancing across the airways
In the sunlight

-Holly Beckwith

Orange sunrises
Bright yellow sun in blue sky
Pink purple sunsets

-Erica Schletz

Surfing on the wind
Cloud castles, St. Elmo's fire
Mountains far below

-Megan Farley

Cross the equator, Ode to Quito
Insane terrain, rapidly rising volcanoes
Luscious greenery plunging deeply
Take my breath away

–Beth Fielder

Northern polar lights
Aurora borealis
Dancing in heaven

–Carolien Libbrecht

At peace in the air
The sky as our own
The foothills appear
Our valley below

–Renee Granata

33

Even the watchful, purple hills
That hold the lake
Could not see so well as I
The stain of evening
Creeping from its heart
Nor the round, yellow eyes of the hamlet
Growing filmy with mists

–Amelia Earhart, "From an Airplane"[19]

[19]Amelia Earhart papers.

3) BLOOD TIES

A single spider's thread
Ties the duckweed
To the shore

–Fukuda Chiyo-ni (1703–1775)[20]

[20]Patricia Donegan, "Chiyo-Ni's Haiku Style," *Simply Haiku: An E-Journal of Haiku and Related Forms,* 2003-2004, http://simplyhaiku.com/SHv2n3/reprints/Patricia_Donegan.html.

"My earliest recollection of the nature of blood ties takes me poolside, to California when I was an age group swimmer for the Mission Viejo Nadadores. Before every swim meet, my mom wrote the initials C.G. on my right upper arm, in waterproof black marker. This was in memory of Carlos Gaspard, my maternal great-grandfather. Gaspard was a swimmer. During his early lifetime, in the town of San Pedro, in Argentina, there were no swimming pools. Competitions were held in the fast-flowing, muddy waters of the Paraná River.

As the river flows, all that swimming represents was passed on by Gaspard to my grandmother, Mabel. She in turn, passed it onto my mom, who then passed it onto me. Blood ties are like these connective threads encompassing the traditions and cultures of both sources of familial ancestry: the people responsible for my genes, and my own intergenerational identity. They represent the past and the future while existing in the present, as we create our own threads to intertwine with the web our ancestors created, in the hopes our legacy will be carried forth too.

This section features a colorful poetic mélange by three generations of pilots. It underscores the ties that bind, the collective spirit we share as women of the skies, and what the world looks like through our eyes from thousands of feet in the air."

The above introduction was written by Captain Pauwels' daughter, Nathalie.

Lighting one candle
With another candle—
Spring evening.

-Yosa Buson (1716-1784)[21]

[21]R.H. Blyth, *Haiku: Vol. 2- Spring,* (Tokyo: Hokuseido Press, 1950), 55.

Yellow gardenia
Each of your seven petals
A world in itself

–Linda Pauwels

Daffodils in bloom
On a downward sloping hill
Above a drainage ditch

-Nathalie Pauwels

Gray-haired chin
Brown, knowing eyes
Old German shepherd

-Linda Pauwels

Bluebird
Crestfallen
Perching in the rain

-Linda Pauwels

Shimmering flaxen threads
Waving playfully in the breeze
Ah? Corgi butt

–Nathalie Pauwels

Flakes dance softly from the clouds
Blanketing the world in silence
From beneath the icy shrouds
A cardinal sings

–Nathalie Pauwels

Araignée du matin: chagrin

Araignée du midi: souci

Araignée du soir: espoir!

French saying, often used by *Marguerite (Maggy) Preud'Homme Pauwels,* my husband's mother, and grandmother to Nathalie. Here is an image of Maggy's pilot logbook, circa 1964.

Pearly red wings
Strength in bloom
Amaryllis

-Linda Pauwels

44

4) VIGNETTES OF RESILIENCE

Bamboo grove—
Here, too, there's no
Perfection

-Kobayashi Issa (1763–1828)[22]

[22]David G. Lanoue, "Haiku of Kobayashi Issa," http://haikuguy.com/issa.

In its purest sense, resilience is the ability of a strained body to recover its original size and shape after being subject to the stress of compression. It is no coincidence the elegant, simple bamboo, a deceptively strong material that bends but does not break, became the bones of early aircraft.[23]

The symbolism of bamboo runs deep in Eastern thought. An understanding of the practical applications of its properties can provide benefits in our everyday lives. The emptiness at the core of bamboo, for example, reflects our ability to train the mind to shut out the noise.

Captain Reyné O'Shaughnessy personally discovered how the practice of meditation serves to buffer the stressors of the job. She became certified in Mindfulness Based Stress Reduction (MBSR) and founded Piloting 2 Wellbeing. These are her thoughts on the topic of resilience:

"Outside of the constricts of concrete thoughts… We adapt.

Life may not come with a clear road map, but everyone will experience its everyday twists and turns, from stresses to traumatic events. Some, with more lasting impact: divorce, the death of a loved one, a serious illness. Each change affects each person differently, bringing a unique flood of thoughts, strong emotions and uncertainty. Most people generally adapt well over time to stressful, life-changing situations—in part thanks to resilience.

As much as resilience involves bouncing back from these difficult experiences, it can also empower personal growth. Becoming more resilient helps us get through difficult circumstances and even improve our lives as we navigate this world of dew."

---

[23]Linda Pauwels, "Bamboo Became the Bones of Early Aircraft," in *The Orange County Register*, September 26, 2004.

The world of dew
Is the world of dew
And yet, and yet...

–Kobayashi Issa (1763–1828)[24]

---

[24]Robert Hass, *The Essential Haiku: Versions of Basho, Buson, and Issa* (Hopewell, NJ: The Ecco Press, 1994), 227-8.

Dear Sir,

Not quite—as yet. But we consider these unusually promising. So please send us some more when you have some you like, perhaps with this card as a reminder.

Yours, H. Monroe

-Rejection Slip. May 16, 1921[25]

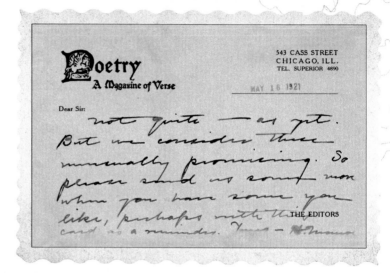

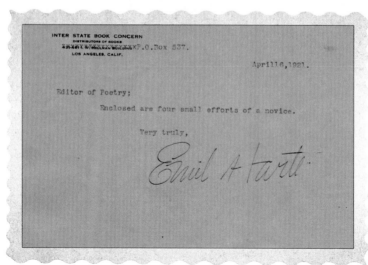

---

[25]Amelia Earhart papers, image number b6f113i8, b6f113i1. [Note: Earhart submitted poems under a male pen name, Emil Harte-Ed.]

Fear of change
Keeps me
In hibernation

-Linda Pauwels

Longing for happiness
Heavy
Sleeping in the rain

-Linda Pauwels

Loneliness hurts
Rocks covered in white
Protected from pain

-Linda Pauwels

A plastic cup in my hand
A piece of cardboard where I stay
I look up at you with defeated eyes
As you look the other way

-Terri McCallister, from "Homeless"

Incorporeal
The wind whips around the trees
They cry out, distressed

-Nathalie Pauwels

I visited the Yard, as fall began
Tall trees greeted me, their long-lost friend
Japanese maples, hinting of red
A twinge of melancholy
In the clean, crisp air
Why do mothers suffer so?
Loving a child, then letting her go
Though another remains, in this empty nest
Family bonds were washed away
By a river of tears

-Linda Pauwels, "Empty Nest"

Summer broken bones
Winter crying still it hurts
I just want to fly

–Pamela Korshin Sperry

I have seen so much
In this solitary life
Not enough to leave

–Terri McCallister

It is the peace of flying the first light of morning
The grace of ascending the moonlit night
The power of perseverance to keep on keeping on
However relentless the fight

–Madeline Ungurain, from "Soar"

Lo único que importa
Es que te sepas
Levantar

–Maciel Mejía, from "No Importa"

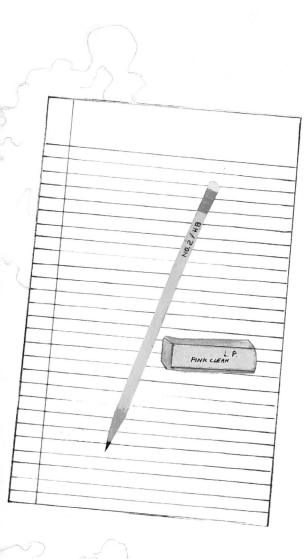

Three hours plus
A pile of eraser-crumbs
Later, a bitter almond under her tongue
She shoves herself away
From the desk, spins
A triple in the chair, stands, stretches
Until she is twenty-three feet tall
Runs out the back door, rolls down
The hill into the woods
Picks squirrels' nests out of trees, hurls them
Up the hill—kicks them
When they bounce down
Rockets back to the house—a meteor trail
Of leaves and sticks
Breaks window-glass into brittle candy
Lands in a closet, locked, suffocating
Pierced by a shard, she deflates, slips
Under the door, flea-size and quick
Skitters up
The side of the desk
Springs
Onto her chair, sighs
Back to shape, and sharpens
Her pencil

-Laureen Miklos, "Pencil and Eraser"

Hustle
Bustle
Racing mind
Fell behind
Is he ok?
Is she ok?
Am I ok?
Can't say
Problems on problems
And stress upon stress
I can't break, but I'll bend
Can you show me the end?
I just want some peace
For the humming to cease
What will it take to quiet the
Noise
Takeoff Checklist
Complete
There it is

-Erica Glanz, "PEACE"

The firstborn child of my mother
Died in a few hours
Does she hold it still
As she might have him
When we fail?

–Amelia Earhart[26]

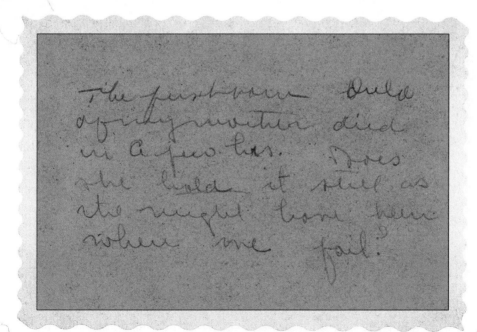

[26]Amelia Earhart papers, image number b6f104i5. [Earhart's mother's miscarriage of a baby girl, caused when she was thrown against the brake lever of a cable car, is discussed in Mary S. Lovell. *The Sound of Wings*. New York: St. Martin's Press, 1989-Ed.]

Like crackling icicles,
Your brittle sword-branches
Rattle in the small breezes
Of thick warm nights

Knowing nothing of cold,
Is it with the malice of ignorance,
That you chill
The thick, warm dreams
Of souls uneasy at discomfort?

–Amelia Earhart, "Palm Tree"[27]

```
            Palm tree.                    b6f113i6

   Like crackling icicles,
   your brittle sword-branches
   rattle in the small breezes
   of thick warm nights.


   Knowing nothing of cold,
   is it with the malice of ignorance,
   that you chill
   the thick,warm dreams
   of souls uneasy at discomfort?
```

[27]Amelia Earhart papers, image number b6f113i6.

Seasons pass and dull the visceral ache
Which morphs into a different pain
One laced with awe at all achieved
In such short time atop the earthly plane

It's said memory returns life
To those no longer with us
Your long brown hair shines in the sun
The wind whispers beneath your wings

–Nathalie Pauwels and Linda Pauwels,
"For Francesca"

This poem is in memory of flight instructor Francesca Norris, who died at age twenty-five, along with her student Yu Qiu, age twenty-two, during a flight training accident in 2019.

The following poems were written in the Spring of 2021, while still in the midst of the COVID-19 pandemic:

Gaze out the window
Gray clouds over sparkly lights
The cabin is still

–Shakar Soltani

Contagion found us
Silence at the terminal
The world stopped spinning

–Bethany Miller

Longing for loved ones
Flying hearts from here to there
Delivering love

-Erica Schletz

We fly without you
And wait for your safe return
Rise now and come back

-Bethany Miller

Enjoy the lockdown
It will be over too soon
Vaccinations loom!

-Carol Scherer

The gallant armada
Sweeps beyond the leaden sky
I fly above the hills
This is mine

-Mary Jo Zignego

No time to be shy
Let's fight and become stronger
Airlines, back to fly!

-Isabel Blanch Matute

Spring is here at last
Like birds learning how to fly
We're back in the sky

—Isabel Blanch Matute

Crocus   Daisy   Bluebell   Lavander

63

5) LOVE OF FLYING

A single butterfly
Fluttering and drifting
In the wind

–Masaoka Shiki (1867-1902)[28]

[28]R.H. Blyth, *A History of Haiku* (Tokyo: Hokuseido Press, 1964). 2: 82.

Why do pilots love to fly? When I asked aviation pioneer Mary Wallace "Wally" Funk how flying made her feel, her reply was: "Fantastic!! I loved every minute of every flight I've taken since age seven."[29]

How it feels to fly can be difficult to put into words, because it means "something different for each of us," wrote WASF Cornelia Fort, shortly before she was killed ferrying an airplane, the first American woman to die on war duty. "I can't say exactly why I fly but I know why as I've never known anything in my life. I know it otherwise than in beauty. I know it in dignity and self-sufficiency and in the pride of skill. I know it in the satisfaction of usefulness."[30]

For high school senior and student pilot Jessica Toddun, the youngest contributor to this book, flying is a magical experience, always beautiful and dreamlike. Indeed, beauty seems to take on another dimension from above. In addition to feeling "powerful and humbled at the same time," Jessica described when she has control and is flying the plane as, "It is like an extension of myself, not just a vehicle for transportation."[31]

Unexpectedly, glimpses of a unitive state come to light when a pilot is as one with the airplane, unable to define where they end and where the machine begins.[32] These moments are like waypoints on a flight plan to the spiritual realm. A realm where poetic words take flight.

---

[29]Mary Wallace Funk, email to author, June 1, 2021. [Subsequent to this email, Wally was selected to join the inaugural crewed flight on Blue Origin, making her the oldest person to fly to space. -Ed.]
[30]Cornelia Fort, "At the Twilight's Last Gleaming," in *Woman's Home Companion*, July, 1943, 19.
[31]Jessica Toddun, email to author, April 25, 2021.
[32] Linda Pauwels, "Flying is the Sweetest Part," in *The Orange County Register,* November 17, 2002.

An Airplane soared into the sky
Ah ! how I wish 'twas you and I,
Forgetting all our woes and cares
In that vast dome away up there !

Just God and blue and you and I
Alone at last beneath the sky.
With carefree mein and wealth untold -
Growing - growing, as our wings unfold.

Dear God thus set our spirits free
To feel Thy wings come nearer me
Forgetting woe and troubled strife
We'd thank Thee Lord, for richer life.

Louise composed this shortly after she "soloed" in Calif. and sent to me. My copy is yellowed with age.

Bill

Image: Louise Thaden papers Smithsonian[33]

---

[33]Louise Thaden, "Untitled poem written after her first solo," 1927, Folder 1, Box 4, Archives Division, National Air and Space Museum, Smithsonian Institution, Washington, DC.

Light blue crystal clear
Gentle swirl of adventure
One butterfly soars

-Melissa Aho, "100 LL"

Wise pilots will tell you
That buying an airplane
Is essentially just adopting
A child

-Ellen Quist

Getting there
Faster
New adventure
The joy of flying
Your own plane

-Delia Jones

Green grass fields below
The yellow cub touches down
A picnic today

–Mary Jo Zignego

I own a Cessna
That Cessna knows it's payday
My Cessna owns me

-Chelsea Frost

My heart is broken
Flying is my great passion
But I am flat broke

-Chelsea Frost

Nothing beats flying
In the morning at sunrise
Except for sleeping

-Chelsea Frost

Zip line screaming fun
Till the tree collided me
Now I cannot fly

-Pamela Korshin Sperry

Soaring graceful high
Feeling like a goddess, I
Need and love the sky

-Pamela Korshin Sperry

Too much coffee
How much time is left?
I check the door camera
Can I be let out?

-Carolee Hanny Brainerd

My weight and balance are out of whack
Now to move my CG forward or aft?
I just want to fly
Why is there so much damn math?

-Courtney Richardson

Dihedral keeps level—perhaps your mind too
Computing air pressures, weight and balance—Oooooh!
And then there's the engine, carb heat, mixture rich
Magnetos, RPM… Son of a b….!

-Suzanne Ramsey, from "On Obtaining a Pilot's License"

Wings wobble bobble
Elevator floats freely
Prop leads me forward

-Tammy LaBarbera

Airspeed alive
Pitch up
Enjoy the view

-Antonella Mancebo

The plane is shaking
Below me is only earth
The high is worth it

-Brittany Himert

Feeling so alive
Soaring like an uncaged bird
Embracing the sky

-Leslie Nixon

Slow flight. Cusp of stall
Throttle, stick work in reverse
Ultimate control

-Sarah Byrn Rickman

Crosswind from the south.
Hard left aileron. Left wheel
Touches grass, Stays down

-Sarah Byrn Rickman

To loop and to roll
Then look at the clouds below
Pilots stay special

-Elizabeth Hawley

Power out, look deep
Please, for God's sake, right rudder
The instructor pleads

-Ellen Quist

Little cloud flies by
A missed approach just for this?
It laughs, "Go around!"

-Megan Farley

I would like to give you the sky
And I would delight in it, to see you
fly, and be happy, and be free
And I would hold you there
In time and in space

–Janet Patton

The earth and all its troubles left
all the things that souls destroy
now heaven bound, oh heaven bound
with pure and soaring joy

Then like an eagle, wings outspread
to look upon the earth below
where all about is light and air
no greater freedom one can know

I try to keep my thoughts quite sane
for no immortal angel I
but must depend on mere machine
that I may thusly fly

–Betty Innes, from "Flying"

75

Can you preflight the plane
Co-pilot?
Can you pre-flight the plane?
And the priming and the timing
Of the fuel for the engine
For the flight that's right in the middle of the night
And the sleep we missed in the spar
And the herk and jerk of the hoist at work
Into the dark of the murky marine layer
Can you preflight the plane
Co-pilot?
Can you pre-flight the plane?

–Elizabeth Booker, from "Night Rescue"

Silver bird takes flight
Soaring high, reaching new height
Quickly out of sight

–Carolee Hanny Brainerd

London, Paris, Brussels, Rome
I can't remember when I left home
I climb in the flight deck to leave earth behind
Always hoping the panel instruments align
The seat, the yoke, the throttles call to me
Feeling the power on the takeoff sets me free

–Pam Catlin, from "My Second Home"

Pinpoints of light
Jet airplane take me home tonight
I see the Orion
I see the Big Dipper
Oh, jet airplane can't you move quicker?
Passing time
What's on my mind
Pinpoints of light
Jet airplane, take me home tonight

–Beth Fielder

Argentina, cuna de mi vida
Qué lindo verte desde arriba
Aterrizando el 787 con una sonrisa emotiva

–Antonella Mancebo

Kiss of the morning dew coats the fabric wings
The quietest part of the morning just before dawn
Another set of wings in the still lake reflection
The trusty companion Husky dog on the tail
Always excited for this type of run
A push and a pull to tug the Avitat in place
An investigative loop around tells me all is just right
A two-step dance from the dock to float
To no one but me I yell "clear prop"
Stillness and silence are at once replaced
Down water rudders leave a temporary trail
With much more water ahead than behind
It's time to soar to the blue sky above

-Tammy LaBarbera, "A Float Flutters the Heart"

Wet grass, calm winds, quiet
Engine coughs, prop spins, wheels move
Runway, power, roll

-Sarah Byrn Rickman

Don't be afraid of the Tail Dragon
The one that's sitting in the back
Tail Dragon wants to be your friend
He rests at a high angle of attack

Once you get his quirky ways
He'll make the world seem fun and new
Nose Dragon will seem a little dull
But that's ok, your skillset grew!

Tail Dragon keeps you on your toes
His favorite word is "rudder"
You'll be all smiles that first time
You grease him in like butter

-Chelsea Frost, "Tail Dragon"

This flying dragon leaves the earth's boundaries
It flies towards the edges of a blackening sky
It soars, it glides, it climbs
Higher than the highest of mountains
It ducks under, around, and over
The darkest clouds
It loves the night sky
Immersed in dancing northern lights
Showered by the remnants of Perseid stars
As it speeds towards the tricky moon

–Gulcin Gilbert, from "Ode to the 777"

Singing zoot suits and parachutes
And wings of silver hue
He'll ferry planes
Like his mama used to do

–Delphine Bohn papers,[34] *adapted from WASP Songbook*[35]

[34]Delphine Bohn papers.
[35]"PBS: American Experience, WASP Songbook," accessed March 10, 2021, https://www.pbs.org/wgbh/americanexperience/features/flygirls-wasp-songbook/.

The tower's "all clear"
A beautiful sky above
The world shines below

Who and where am I?
Just a girl who likes to fly
Speeding in the sky

-Raquel Ramsey, haiku written in memory of
WASP Nadine Ramsey.

6) Finding Balance

Exhausted I sought
a country inn, but found
wisteria in bloom

–Matsuo Basho (1644–1694)[36]

[36]Sam Hamill, *The Sound of Water: Haiku by Basho, Buson, Issa and Other Poets* (Boston: Shambhala, 2011), 10.

"Aviators are unique beings. At home we talk about flying, and while flying we talk about home. We are ever on the lookout for the only thing that will give us balance—family, friends, and communities who support our need to fly and the lifestyle that comes with it. This life is like no other.

We pilots are made of determination and light. We are grit and joy. We reach forward for the next liftoff, while at the same time reaching back to offer a hand to those who will follow in our footsteps. Because the road to the sky was long and hard, and ever takes its toll.

Balance–that elusive union of wonderment and reality, of sweat and joy, of earth and sky. It's tempering the work with the spiritual. Flying is both a calling and a passion. And it's only made possible by those who keep us grounded while letting us soar."

The introduction for this final chapter was written by social scientist Bethany Miller, DBA, who is also a retired Southwest Airlines pilot and Lt Col, USAF (Ret).

Out her office window
Blue sky beckons

She lifts her flight bag
Pearls tossed at the bottom

Bugle echoes
Across the airfield

She starts the propeller
Headed toward sunset

Golden rays radiate
Off distant city glass

She tilts her wing
Waving at her reflection

-Kristi Feinzig

I have missed hugs and first-time steps
But others have done the same
The ones I have are just as sweet
A part of playing the game

My children and spouse have shared my dreams
It really is worth the while it seems
My wish for all is to do what is best
To work hard and go after your quest

-Kathleen Cosand, from untitled poem

My head's in the clouds
And when my airplane follows
It keeps me grounded

-Donna Miller

Awake in the night
As I count: five, seven. Five
Haiku is alive!

-Carol Scherer

Eyes close for the night
The frogs serenade me loudly
Captive audience

-Nathalie Pauwels

Dark and dreary I taxi
But a BINOVC means I will need
My sunglasses soon

-Susan McDonald

How to find balance
Need to add more, right rudder
Oh yes—That is it!

-Laurie Parenteau

Left wing or right wing
Airplanes need both wings to fly
Peace on earth and sky

-Laurie Parenteau

Blue sky meets black road
Between this plane I travel
To a temporary home

-Nathalie Pauwels

Love retirement
But I miss other pilots
Much more than flying

-Carol Scherer

In a job saturated by rules
Regulations, and men
I used my hard-earned skills
Of flying and humor
To fit in

-Kathy Shelton, from "Flying"

We'll do it like the airlines, as we do every day
Switch flying each leg is the easiest way

Now many of you know that's easier said than done
When aforementioned spouse is Type A number one

We found out from the start through trial and error
Letting him fly causes him much less terror

Before you think our flying together is grim—it's not.
You have to know the partner you've got

It's give and take in flying and in life
If you really stand a chance as husband and wife

-Kelly Jeffries, from "Two Pilots, One Plane"

An odd loneliness
In a life such as this
One I chose to do long ago
Because flying is such bliss

I'll see you soon my dear
Keep the home fires burning
On the other side of night
As the world keeps turning

–Terri McCallister, from "And Through it All, There is You"

I am so hurt. My heart? It's broken!
Love departs from me…
My heart cries for help
Maybe one day it too will walk away
I hear the voices of my heart weeping
Love depart from me

–Bethoyia Powell, from "Love Depart from Me"

Quiero sudar
y bailar un tango más
y morir así quizá
Abrazada a ti

–Lucía Aránega Abellán

He has seen clearly
Therefore
Irony is his displeasure
His humor
And his tenderness

–Amelia Earhart, "My Friend"[37]

```
                    My Friend.

He has seen clearly;
Therefore
irony is his displeasure
his humor,
and his tenderness.
```

[37] Amelia Earhart papers, image number b6f113i7.

To M ——— .

Like your body's beauty
the humor of your frankness
pleased them—— who saw the surface only,
nor saw you
laughing at them with a wistful scorn
and eyes of cool intelligence.

Like your body's beauty
The humor of your frankness
Pleased them—who saw the surface only
Nor saw you
Laughing at them with a wistful scorn
The eyes of cool intelligence

-Amelia Earhart, "To M"[38]

---

[38]Amelia Earhart papers, image number b6f113i5.

The light from the window
Falls on your becoming
Green sweater
With your brown hair
& up tilted nose
You are very American

–Amelia Earhart[39]

[39]Amelia Earhart papers, image number b6f104i6.

We are going on an adventure
Souls on board plus one
Shh just you and me know
Take off V1 rotate
I can feel you're excited
Hurray!
We can touch the sky
Climb and maintain
Look at the wonders God has made
I promise to guide you
Hug you and keep you safe
We've got Daddy, God, and our faith
We will fly again
Someday soon, I know
Meanwhile let's just enjoy
Landing checklist
I'll carefully hang my wings
Can't wait to hold you, my prince

-Jacqueline Pulido, "My Little Passenger"

I knew his eyes were blue
In my womb, as he grew
Enveloped in the hopes and dreams
Of his mother-to-be
Generations of mothers and fathers past
All living inside me
The searing pain of childbirth
Doused by tears of joy
Gave way to an indescribable feeling
The first time I held my baby boy
His handsome face, close to mine
Confirmed what I already knew
As his gaze met mine, I saw his eyes
They were unmistakably blue

-Linda Pauwels, "Blue"

The following poem was sent via text message by my adult son, on March 10, 2021,
for my fifty-eighth birthday:

I look into the Sky Blue
That sky that was never the limit
For you
You taught me strength
Never changed your hue
You taught me wisdom
You kept me true
I know our skies
Were never always blue
Just know I love you

-Patrick Pauwels

Ready for takeoff
She fought the good fight, kept faith
See you in heaven

-Jacqueline Pulido

Uplifting her wings
Little Skyhawk bring me close
Sister sense me here

-Lynsey Steinberg

Within the fish-eye
Lens of sky
Slowly a plane circles
Come, join me

-Delia Jones

Mountains and beaches
A place with the best of worlds
Take me there, I'll stay

-Celeste Pearce

Give me open blue
Anywhere wind will take me
Pilot or pirate

–Kristin Sito

Shooting stars above
Dreaming of what we could be
Living what we are

–Carolien Libbrecht

Zulu time runs here
A melody clear of clouds
Hope blooms in the sun

–Melissa Aho, "Zulu Time"

What a lovely day
Earth's shadow disappearing
Yesterday is gone

–Carolien Libbrecht

Brilliant color bands
Span the darkening blue sky
As dusk closes in
Stars begin to shine brightly
A full moon rises
We cannot outfly the night

–Carolee Hanny Brainerd, "Racing the Night"

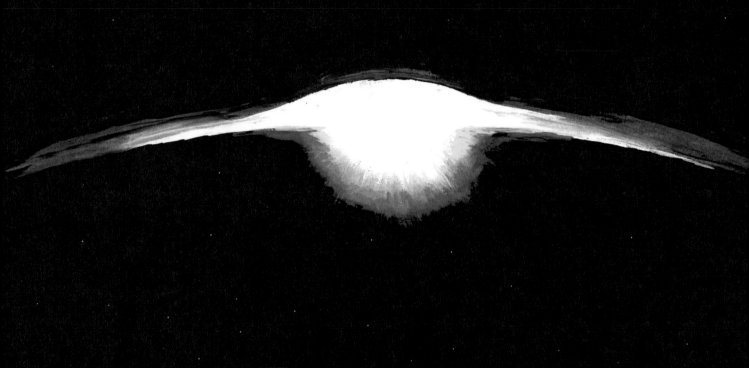

POSTSCRIPT

Learn first, O cloud, the road that thou must go
Then hear my message ere thou speed away
Before thee mountains rise and rivers flow
When thou art weary, on the mountains stay
And when exhausted, drink the rivers' driven spray

–Kalidasa (5th century CE), from "The Cloud Messenger"[40]

[40]Kalidasa, "The Cloud Messenger," in *Kalidasa, Translations of Shakuntala, and Other Works*, trans. Arthur W. Ryder (New York: E.P. Dutton and Co., 1914), 187. https://www. sacred-texts.com.

Appendix: How to Write a Haiku

Traditional Japanese haiku is a short poem of seventeen syllables, arranged in three lines in a 5/7/5 syllable format. It often focuses on images of nature, expressed simply and with intensity. Haiku written in other languages have developed their own styles and traditions while incorporating aspects of the original haiku form.

If you enjoyed our shared creative efforts in *Women Pilots Write Poetry* and would like to try your hand at haiku, here are some suggestions and resources to get you started:

First, for the adults only, resolve to purposely set aside what you've learned. Then, attempt to transport yourselves back in time to when you were children, to regain a semblance of a "beginner's mind." This refers to an attitude of openness, devoid of filters and preconceived notions.[41] Taking a closer look at the illustrations in the book may help with this exercise.

Keeping this *tabula rasa* as a backdrop, begin with utmost simplicity:

1) Line one: Describe a setting.
Example: *a bumpy ride*

2) Line two: Describe a subject.
Example: *the whole plane*

3) Line three: Describe an action.
Example: *pretending*

---

[41]David G. Lanoue, *Write Like Issa: A Haiku How-to* (New Orleans: HaikuGuy.com, 2017).

a bumpy ride
the whole plane
pretending

The above haiku was composed for *Women Pilots Write Poetry* by David G. Lanoue, professor of English at Xavier University of Louisiana and former president of the Haiku Society of America. He also offered readers a bit of wisdom:

"In recent years, I've become more and more convinced that haiku is an art of discovery. By opening one's heart and mind to the present moment, the poet discovers something. It's not like the poet is thinking, "Here's an idea; now let me frame it in haiku form." It's more like: "I'm experiencing and/or remembering this moment deeply and catching it as a haiku: let's see what I might discover…"[42]

Resources for further haiku exploration:

The Haiku Foundation education resources: *https://thehaikufoundation.org/learn/the-haiku-foundation-education-wall/*

Haiku Society of America educational resources: *https://www.hsa-haiku.org/education.htm*

---

[42]Lanoue, personal emails to the author, January 19, 2021 and July 5, 2021.

BIBLIOGRAPHY

Blyth, R.H. *A History of Haiku: Vol. 2.* Tokyo: Hokuseido Press, 1964.

Blyth, R.H. *Haiku: Vol. 2- Spring.* Tokyo: Hokuseido Press, 1950.

Bohn, Delphine. Papers. History of Aviation Collection. Special Collections and Archives Division, Eugene McDermott Library, The University of Texas at Dallas.

Donegan, Patricia. "Chiyo-Ni's Haiku Style." *Simply Haiku: An E-Journal of Haiku and Related Forms.* 2003-2004. http://simplyhaiku.com/SHv2n3/reprints/Patricia_Donegan.html.

Earhart, Amelia. Papers. George Palmer Putnam Collection. MSP 9. Purdue University Archives and Special Collections, Purdue University Libraries.

Fort, Cornelia. "At the Twilight's Last Gleaming." *Woman's Home Companion*, July, 1943.

Hamill, Sam. *The Sound of Water: Haiku by Basho, Buson, Issa and Other Poets.* Boston: Shambhala, 2011.

Hass, Robert. *The Essential Haiku: Versions of Basho, Buson, and Issa.* Hopewell, NJ: The Ecco Press, 1994.

Lanoue, David G. "Haiku of Kobayashi Issa." http://haikuguy.com/issa.

Lanoue, David G. *Write Like Issa: A Haiku How-to*, New Orleans: HaikuGuy.com, 2017.

Lyall, Gavin. *Freedom's Battle Volume II: The War in the Air 1939-1945*. London: Hutchinson Random House, 2007.

MacKail, J.W. *The Eclogues of Virgil.* New York: Modern Library, 1934. http://www.sacred-texts.com.

Morris, Sammie L. "What Archives Reveal: The Hidden Poems of Amelia Earhart." *Libraries Research Publications*, Paper 28, November, 2006, http://docs.lib.purdue.edu/lib_research/28.

Pauwels, Linda. "Bamboo Became the Bones of Early Aircraft." *The Orange County Register*, September 26, 2004.

Pauwels, Linda. "Flying is the Sweetest Part." *The Orange County Register*, November 17, 2002.

Pauwels, Linda. "Jet's Thrust Starts with A Big Breath In." *The Orange County Register*, May 30, 2004.

Ryder, Arthur W. *Kalidasa, Translations of Shakuntala, and Other Works.* New York: E.P. Dutton and Co., 1914. https://www. sacred-texts.com.

Thaden, Louise. Writings. Untitled Poem, First Solo. 1927. NASM.XXXX.0006-M0000088-0020. Louise McPhetridge Thaden Collection. Archives Division, National Air and Space Museum, Smithsonian Institution, Washington, D.C.

Wright, Richard. Haiku: *This Other World.* New York: Arcade Publishing, 1998.

Beyond Haiku: Women Pilots Write Poetry

Contributing Authors:

This is an alphabetical list of contributors, type of flying, and location (with country of origin added in parenthesis). Airports, where listed for airline pilots, use the three letter IATA station code. Additional information about the authors may be found on the book's website www.beyondhaiku.com.

Aho, Melissa, Student Pilot, Minnesota, USA

Aránega Abellán, Lucía, A330/350 First Officer, MAD

Beckwith, Holly, B737 Captain (Ret), MIA

Blanch Matute, M. Isabel, A330 Captain, MAD

Blue, Syd, Commercial Pilot, California, USA

Booker, Elizabeth, Helicopter Pilot, United States Coast Guard (Ret)

Brainerd, Carolee Hanny, B787 First Officer, ORD

Catlin, Pam, B737 Captain, ORD

Cosand, Kathleen, B767 First Officer (Ret), DFW

David, Samantha, Private Pilot, Haute-Vienne, France (United Kingdom)

Earhart, Amelia, Aviation Pioneer (1897-1937/39)

Farley, Megan, DHC-8 First Officer (Ret), MDT

Feinzig, Kristi, Student Pilot, Massachusetts, USA

Fielder, Beth, B737 First Officer, MIA

Frost, Chelsea, Commercial Pilot, BLI

Glanz, Erica, Pilot, United States Navy

Gilbert, Gulcin, A320 Captain, LAX

Granata, Renee, Private Pilot, Connecticut, USA

Hawley, Elizabeth, Private Pilot, Texas, USA

Himert, Brittany, Student Pilot, Nevada, USA

Innes, Betty, Private Pilot, Ontario, Canada

Jeffries, Kelly, B737 Captain, ORD

Jones, Delia, Private Pilot, Victoria, Australia

LaBarbera, Tammy, B777 Captain (Ret), AUH

Libbrecht, Carolien, A320 Captain, BRU

Mancebo, Antonella, Flight Instructor, Florida, USA (Argentina)

McCallister, Terri, B737 Captain, DFW

McDonald, Susan, Private Pilot, California, USA

Mejía, Maciel, Aspiring Pilot, San José, Costa Rica

Miklos, Laureen, Helicopter Pilot, United States Navy (Ret)

Miller, Bethany, Former Airline Pilot and United States Air Force Pilot (Ret)

Miller, Donna, B787 First Officer, ORD

Nixon, Leslie, Recreational Pilot, Florida, USA

Oliva, Raquel, Former Student Pilot, Flight Simulator Technician, Florida, USA

O'Shaugnessy, Reyné, B767 Captain, MEM

Parenteau, Laurie, Former Airline Pilot, California, USA

Patton, Janet, B737 Captain, DFW

Pauwels, Nathalie, Flight Instructor, Florida, USA

Pearce, Celeste, B777 First Officer, LGA

Petitt, Karlene, A350 First Officer, SEA

Powell, Bethoyia, B737 First Officer, DFW (Jamaica)

Pulido, Jacqueline, A320 Captain, MEX

Quist, Ellen, Commercial Pilot, Minnesota, USA

Ramsey, Raquel, Retired Educator and Author, California, USA

Ramsey, Suzanne, Private Pilot, Ontario, Canada

Richardson, Courtney, Commercial Pilot, Utah, USA

Rickman, Sarah Byrn, Sport Pilot, Colorado, USA

Scherer, Carol, B777 First Officer (Ret), DFW

Schletz, Erica, B737 First Officer, SLC

Shelton, Kathy, B737 Captain, LAX

Sito, Kristin, Flight Instructor, Colorado, USA

Soltani, Shakar, Student Pilot, Texas, USA

Sperry, Pamela Korshin, A320 Captain, LGA

Steinberg, Lynsey, Student Pilot, Georgia, USA

Thaden, Louise, Aviation Pioneer (1905-1979)

Toddun, Jessica, Student Pilot, California, USA

Ungurain, Madeline, Commercial Student Pilot, British Columbia, Canada

Zignego, Mary Jo, A320 Captain (Ret), DFW

Contributing Artists:

Kryszat, Christine, artist, Connecticut, USA

Patel, Dipesh, A320 First Officer, CLT

Patterson, Priscilla, ASAA aviation artist, Idaho, USA

Pauwels, Nathalie, Flight Instructor, Florida, USA

Petitt, Karlene, A350 First Officer, SEA

Steinberg, Lynsey, medical illustrator, Georgia, USA

Young Artists:

Alley, Sloan, 18, Florida, USA

Batha, Jude, 7, Texas, USA

Catlin, Natalie, 10, Wisconsin, USA

Chabot, Callista, 17, New Hampshire, USA

Downard, Sophia, 16, Arizona, USA

García-Verdugo Blanch, Leilani, 8, Granada, Spain

García-Verdugo Blanch, Leo, 8, Granada, Spain

Govin, Jacob, 10, Texas, USA

Govin, Joseph, 10, Texas, USA

Graver, Lily, 13, Tennessee, USA

Johnson, Kinley, 13, Texas, USA

Molina, Sebastian, 11, Florida, USA

O'Malley, Scarlett, 13, Florida, USA

Peitz, Rebecca, 16, Florida, USA

Pfeiffer, Fiona, 11, Florida, USA

Robinson, Collin, 10, Florida, USA

Rojas-Bolaños, Natalia, 8, Ciudad de Mexico, Mexico

Rose, Phoenix, 13, Colorado, USA

Ruhland, Kennedy, 17, Texas, USA

Ruiz, Giullianna, 11, Puerto Vallarta, Mexico

Somarriba-Barrientos, Grace, 13, Florida, USA

Stauffer, Skye, 15, Texas, USA

Strand, Meghan, 15, South Carolina, USA

Streng, Jazelle, 10, Michigan, USA

Streng, Zoe, 10, Michigan USA

Ugarte Márquez, Isabela, 12, Cuernavaca, Mexico

Illustration Credits

About the cover:

The cover, depicting a monarch butterfly on the nose cone of a Boeing 787, was conceived by the author based on the following haiku by Holly Beckwith (Captain, American Airlines, retired):

Little butterfly
Sunning on the nose cone
Of the jumbo jet

The haiku is representative of the style of Japanese master Kobayashi Issa. The cover emphasis is on simplicity, in keeping with haiku principles. It is evocative of opposing forces: hard, soft; temporal, spiritual; long-lasting, short-lived; masculine, feminine; beauty: of the natural world and that which is man-made.

Artist Callista Chabot, age seventeen, illustrated the cover. She was mentored by Priscilla Patterson, Fellow, American Society of Aviation Artists. The cover design was courtesy of Lynsey Steinberg, MSMI, CMI, Center for Instructional Innovation at Augusta University, in Augusta, Georgia.

About the cameo portraits:

The portraits of Amelia Earhart, Louise Thaden, Delphine Bohn, and Nadine Ramsey are artistic renderings courtesy of artist Priscilla Patterson. They were derived from the study of photographs in circulation. Permission was not required for renderings of Earhart and Thaden, but was obtained for Bohn from the University of Texas as Dallas, and for Ramsey courtesy of the Ramsey family.

Illustrations are listed below by artist name and page number in order of appearance. More information about the artists may be found on the book's website: beyondhaiku.com.

Illustrations:

Amaryllis collage:

ABOUT THE AUTHOR

Captain Linda Pauwels is an airline pilot. For over three decades she has flown thousands of hours, on many types of big airplanes, all over the world. Linda even counts some aviation "firsts" attached to her name. At present, she instructs and evaluates pilots as a check airman on the Boeing 787 for American Airlines.

Linda was born in San Pedro, Buenos Aires, Argentina. She came to the United States at age six, after the death of her father. Having experienced adversity early on in life, she grew to understand and appreciate the value of resilience. Linda integrates intuition and sensitivity, along with a graduate academic preparation in education, in her professional life.

In the mid-2000s, Linda wrote a regular column, titled *From the Cockpit*, for the Orange County Register. She has been secretly writing poetry for a while. Unfortunately, that cat is now out of the bag.

Linda has been married to Frederick, also a pilot, for forty years. They have two adult children, Nathalie and Patrick, domestic animals, and an Asian garden with a bird feeder. The family is scattered around the U.S., with a primary base in North Texas, near DFW airport and a secondary base in South Florida, near MIA.

Books in this Series:

Beyond Haiku: Pilots Write Poetry

Beyond Haiku: Seasons of a Pilot's Life (coming soon)

Beyond Haiku: Military Pilots Write Poetry (coming soon)

Made in United States
North Haven, CT
16 April 2022